THE SAYINGS OF LUZEMILY
The 7-Year Old Sage

Luzemily Prosper

First Edition

Global Publishing Company • Los Angeles, California

THE SAYINGS OF LUZEMILY
The 7-Year Old Sage

Luzemily Prosper

Book layout design and cover design by Charles Prosper

LIBRARY OF CONGRESS CATALOG CARD DATA

ISBN–13 978-0-943845-19-7

PRINTED IN THE UNITED STATES OF AMERICA

12   11   10   9   8   7   6   5   4   3   2   1

Dedicated to Natalia, my dear cousin

Contents

Luzemily Prosper
The 7-Year Old Sage

INTRODUCTION

I remember the day well. Luzemily had just made 7 years old. We began to talk about a fight she had when a little girl her same age attacked her. Knowing self defense from a very young age, she adeptly defended herself – but suddenly she said,

"When I hurt someone, I feel bad - hurting other people is really hurting yourself." – *Luzemily (7 years old)*

Her statement was so sudden, so unexpected, so true and so profound that it really caught me by surprise.

And, from her 7th year onwards, that was the beginning of an unending series of wise sayings that she has been uttering for the last four years. Realizing what was happening, I began to record her pearls of wisdom about a year later.

This little book chronicles four years and some amazing things that Luzemily has said up to the present day. It covers profound thoughts as well as humorous ones that she has said from ages 8 through 11 years old. She is presently 11.

Yes, I am a proud papa, but you will see that it is due to no exaggerated ego. What you will read here in this little book, will serve as thoughts to meditate on for years to come. Enjoy.

Charles Prosper
July 4, 2010

The Sayings of Luzemily

(an anthology)

On Life and Death

You can't stop life from killing you.

– *Luzemily Prosper*
 (8 years old)

On The Nature of Secrets

When only you know something, it's a secret. Once you tell someone else, it's no longer a secret.

— Luzemily Prosper
  (9 years old)

4

On The Nature of God

God is having a dream about us, and we are (like God) having a dream about ourselves.

– Luzemily Prosper
  (10 years old)

On The Purpose of Life

We only have 2 purposes for being on Earth: 1) Is to love and to serve, and 2) To reproduce. Not everyone can do the second, but we all have to do the first.

— *Luzemily Prosper*
(10 years old)

On The Truth of Lying

Everybody lies, and that is the honest truth. And for some reason, everybody has to lie sometimes.

– Luzemily Prosper
   (10 years old)

On Dealing with Bullies

If you fight with words, it's not going to do anything but get your butt kicked.

– Luzemily Prosper
  (10 years old)

On Good and Bad Luck

There is no such thing as good luck or bad luck – only how you think of yourself.

– Luzemily Prosper
(10 years old)

On Thunder & Lightning

It is better to hear thunder than to be hit by lightning.

– Luzemily Prosper
  (10 years old)

A Question On Allergies

Luzemily - Daddy, can a person be allergic to anything?
Dad - Yes.
Luzemily - Well, can a person be allergic to himself?

— Luzemily Prosper
(10 years old)

On Problem Solving

There is a remedy for everything.

– *Luzemily Prosper*
(10 years old)

On Doing Good Things

*When you do good
things, good things
happen.*

*— Luzemily Prosper
(10 years old)*

On Making Mistakes

Life is interesting when you make mistakes because you can always find corrections.

— Luzemily Prosper
   (10 years old)

On The Legality of Hugging

If it was illegal to hug– nobody would be happy.

– *Luzemily Prosper*
  (10 years old)

An Affirmation of Power

"I believe in the power of believing."

– Luzemily Prosper
(10 years old)

A Question of Fruit

Do kiwis eat kiwis?

— *Luzemily Prosper*
  (10 years old)

A Duck Vampire

What do you call a duck vampire?
– Count Quackula

– Luzemily Prosper
(10 years old)

A Dangerous Reptile

What do you call a dangerous reptile on drugs?
– A Crack-odile

– Luzemily Prosper
(10 years old)

On Animal Breeding

If a bull and a dog do it - do you get a bulldog?

*— Luzemily Prosper
(10 years old)*

A Dialogue With Dad

**Dad** - _Luzemily, do you have any idea how much I love you?_
**Luzemily** - _Yes, I can feel the "daddyness"._

– Luzemily Prosper
(10 years old)

An Urgent Request to Dad

Daddy. Hug me. I'm a 'hugaholic'.

— Luzemily Prosper
  (10 years old)

Luzemily's Wit

Dad - You listen to me.

Luzemily - No, you listen to me.

Dad - I'm older.

Luzemily - Yes, but I'm older in coolness.

– Luzemily Prosper
(10 years old)

On The Nature of Time

Time is movement, and if there is no movement, there is no time.

— Luzemily Prosper
  (11 years old)

On The Nature of Space

*There is no such thing
as space. There is
always some molecule
squished together in
space.*

*— Luzemily Prosper
(11 years old)*

On Faith

Always keep your faith up.

— *Luzemily Prosper*
  (11 years old)

On Life

Life is not short if you spend it well.

— *Luzemily Prosper*
  (11 years old)

On Perfect People

If everybody was perfect then nobody would be perfect.

– Luzemily Prosper
(11 years old)

On Horrible Things

There is no such thing as horrible. It's just an opinion.

— *Luzemily Prosper*
   (11 years old)

On The Fairness of Life

Life is unfair only if we think it's unfair.

— *Luzemily Prosper*
  (11 years old)

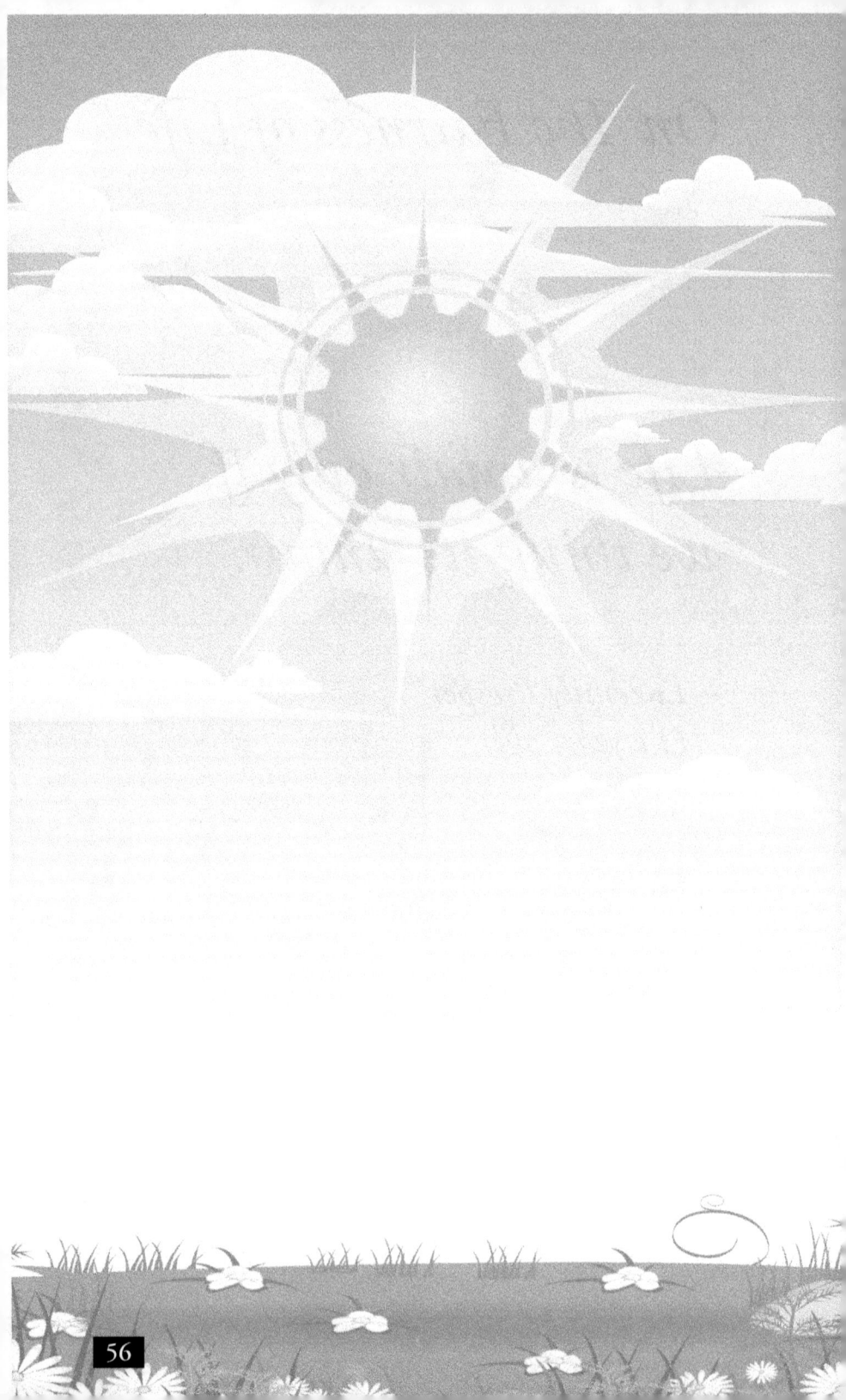

On Believing

Don't believe something you don't want to believe.

– *Luzemily Prosper*
  (11 years old)

On Cartoon Characters

Why does every cartoon character in every episode wear the same clothes?

– *Luzemily Prosper*
  (11 years old)

The 3 Essentials of Life

Three things that you need: keys, faith and your cell phone.

– Luzemily Prosper
(11 years old)

On Begging

Begging is for losers.

– Luzemily Prosper
(11 years old)

Playing The Game of Life

What's the point in playing the game if you are going to win all the time?

— *Luzemily Prosper*
  (11 years old)

On Constant Fighting

Fighting just hurts the soul - the fighting that never stops.

– Luzemily Prosper
   (11 years old)

On Weird People

Nobody is weird;
everybody is unique.

– Luzemily Prosper
  (11 years old)

On Being Born Again

*You are born again
every time you wake
up.*

— *Luzemily Prosper
(11 years old)*

On Moderation

You should have moderation with moderation.

— Luzemily Prosper
(11 years old)

On Being Millionaires

If everyone was a millionaire then no one would be a millionaire.

— *Luzemily Prosper*
  (11 years old)

A Business Success Secret

What are you doing that they're not trying?

— Luzemily Prosper
  (11 years old)

Why Problems Exist

Luzemily - *There's a reason for problems.*
Dad - *Why?*
Luzemily - *To solve them.*
Dad - *Why solve them?*
Luzemily - *For the fun of it.*

— *Luzemily Prosper*
  (11 years old)

On Forcing Others

You can't force anybody to do anything they don't want to do - well, you can, in physical ways but not in mental ways.

— *Luzemily Prosper*
  (11 years old)

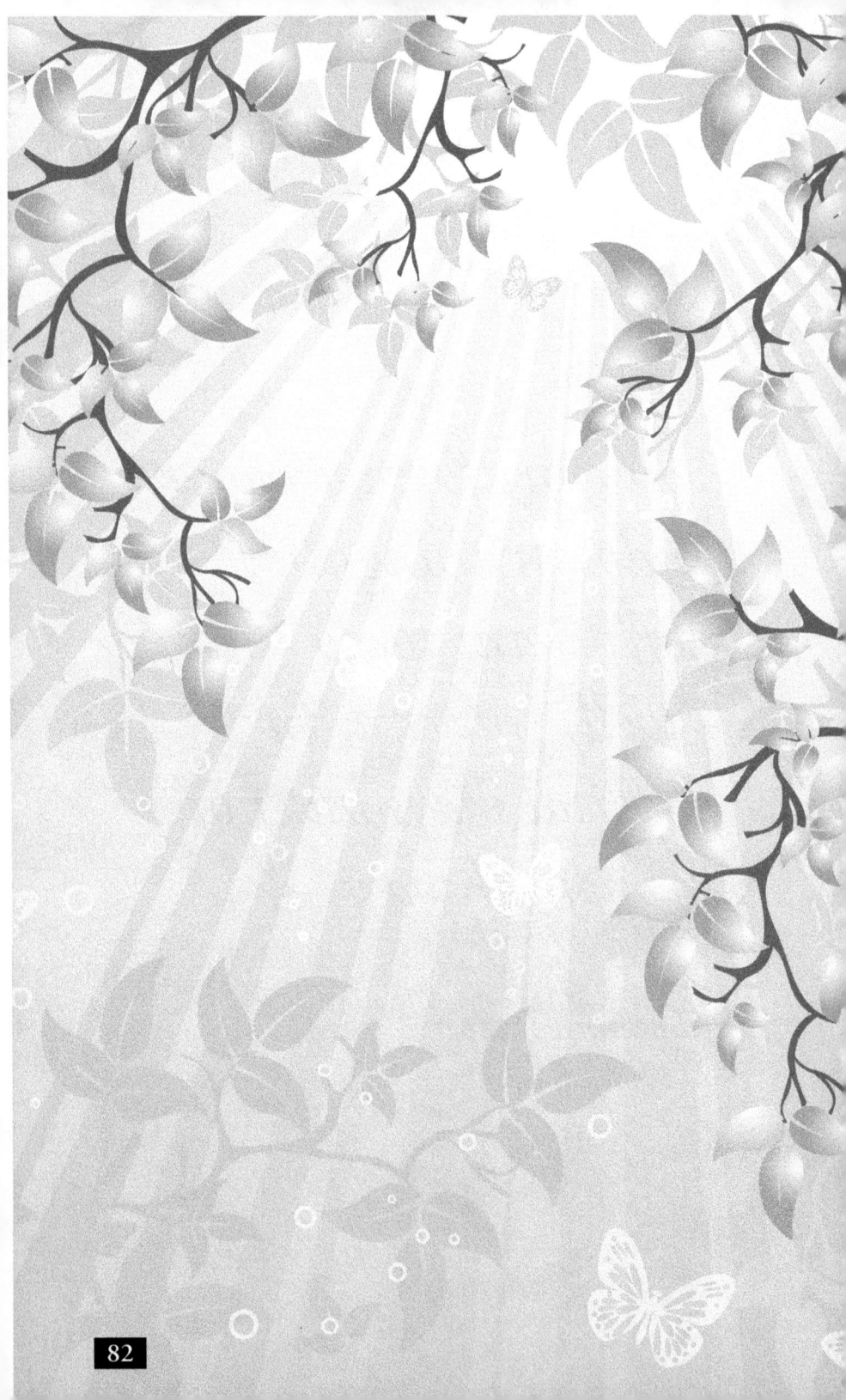

82

A Request vs. A Command

Never ask a command.

– Luzemily Prosper
 (11 years old)

Try, Try Again...

If at first you don't succeed, try, try again – but don't try <u>too</u> hard.

– Luzemily Prosper
  (11 years old)

Adjectives

Every adjective is an opinion.

— *Luzemily Prosper*
  (11 years old)

On Changing Others

You cannot change a person. You can only help.

– *Luzemily Prosper*
   (11 years old)

What Is Money?

Money is an emotion. It can be anything you want it to be.

— Luzemily Prosper
  (11 years old)

Happiness vs. Love

There is a difference between happiness and love. Happiness can be with only one person. Love has to be accompanied by something or someone.

— Luzemily Prosper
(11 years old)

On Problems

*To every problem,
there is a benefit.*

*– Luzemily Prosper
(11 years old)*

Can You Imagine...?

Can you imagine imagining? Can you love loving?

– *Luzemily Prosper*
  (11 years old)

What You Want To Hear

You want to hear what you believe.

— Luzemily Prosper
(11 years old)

On Asking A Question

If you ask a question, you have to be prepared for the answer.

– Luzemily Prosper
(11 years old)

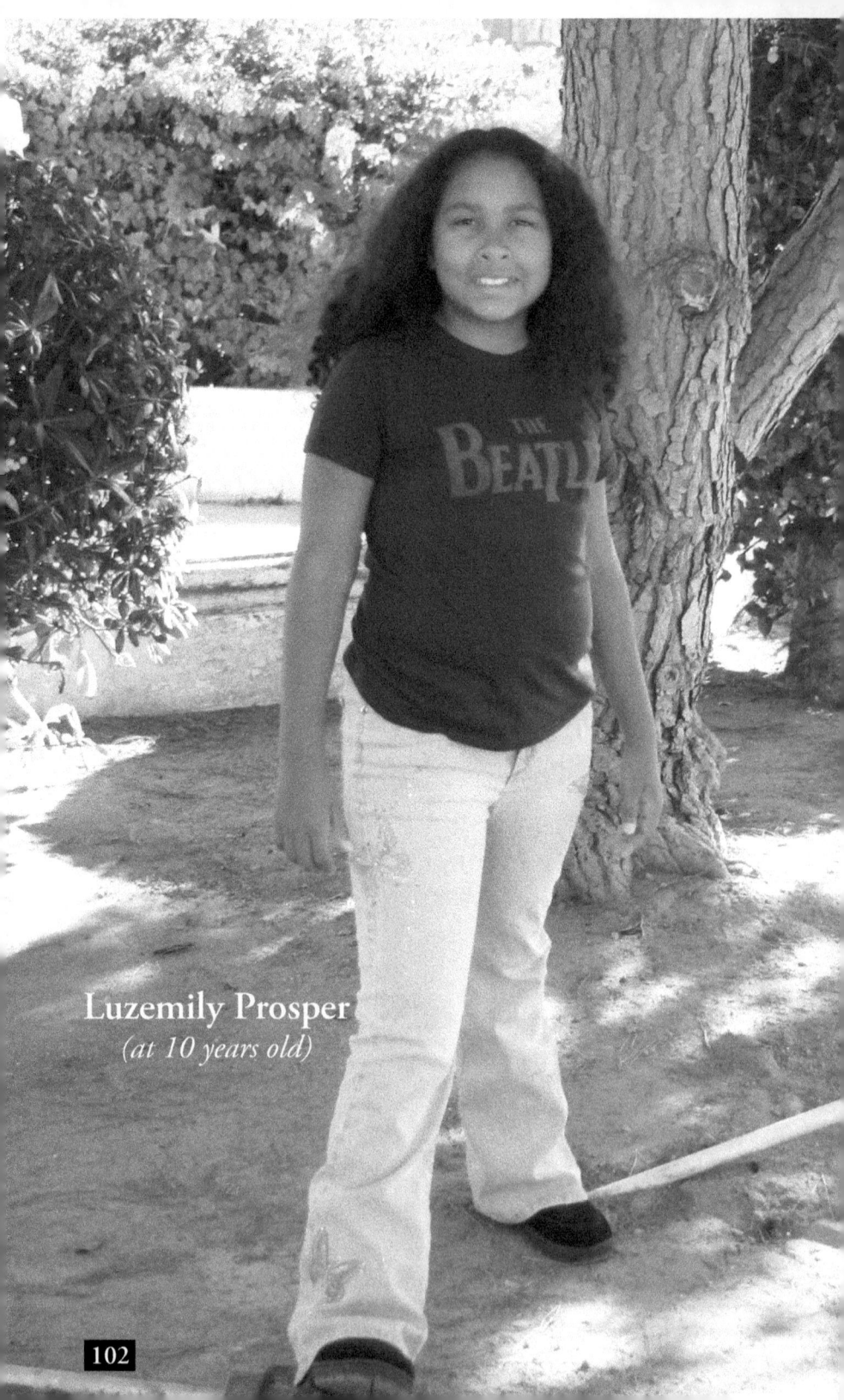

Luzemily Prosper
(at 10 years old)

About The Author

Luzemily Prosper is just like any, straight-A, middle school student. She can be silly and playful, but there is an aspect of her that nobody can ascertain where it comes from, that when she speaks, some pretty profound things come out of those pretty little lips. *(Presently, she is 11 years old – and becoming wiser with each passing year.)*

If you would like to drop Luzemily a line and thank her for her first work or if you would like to order additional copies, you can do so to:

Luzemily Prosper
c/o Global Publishing Company
P.O. Box 29699
Los Angeles, CA 90029
cprosper@prosperballoons.com

www.ingramcontent.com/pod-product-compliance
Lightning Source LLC
Chambersburg PA
CBHW060039040426
42331CB00032B/1434